Fun Things To Do In Retirement

Discover How to Combat Bc
Explore Creative and Adver
Life | More than 67 Ways
Monotony to

By Terrance Torrington

Table of Contents

INTRODUCTION

Depending on what you decide to do with your retirement, it could be a chance to reconnect with your greatest passions and goals. You can try out new things. You may learn new skills and spend more time with the people and activities you enjoy. All of it is up to you.

You no longer have to worry about meeting deadlines at work as a retiree. You are free to have fun and act in any way you want. In addition, even if your income is lower than when you worked full time, you can take advantage of a wide range of senior discounts and be free of debts like credit card debt, a mortgage, and student loans.

There is a lot to gain in retirement. A Merrill Lynch survey uncovered people feel more joyful and less stressed in retirement than at some other time in their grown-up lives.

During a person's working life, leisure often means taking a break from routine and relaxing. However, it's more important to be active and social in retirement. As a result, this book has developed a wide range of activities that can help you stay physically and mentally active in social and fulfillment opportunities.

But remember, freedom and choice are at the heart of retirement. Use these concepts as a starting point to design your course of action!

My neighbor Joyce was forced to retire earlier than planned. She was within three years of wanting to quit, anyway. So, when her job and role were no longer needed, it came as a bit of a shock to her. What next? That was the question she had to find a solution to, and try to fill the remaining hours of the day. She felt lost and a little depressed as retirement approached.

Her husband was by her side. She did not have to look for a new job to supplement their income because with her husband, they had made financial plans for their retirement. However, she had thought little about what she would do to keep herself occupied in her retirement.

It might be appealing not to go to work anymore, but as anyone who has been through lockdown knows, freedom can be a double-edged sword. It would help if you tried to see retirement not as the end of something but as the beginning of something new, because boredom often follows shortly after retirement.

The question is, what are some enjoyable retirement activities? This book is here to help you learn that.

The first piece of advice is to plan for retirement. Be the age you want to look, not the age that others might think you should be. Include new experiences in your retirement planning to prolong your youthfulness.

CHAPTER 1

RETIREMENT AND YOU

What Is Retirement?

When we leave the labor force behind forever, that is retirement. In most developed nations, including the United States, the traditional retirement age is 65. Many countries also have a national pension or benefits system to enhance retirees' incomes. For instance, since 1935, the Social Security Administration (SSA) has been providing monthly income benefits to retirees under the Social Security program in the United States. Other first-world countries also do the same to support seniors in enjoying their retirement life.

Understanding Retirement

Age 62 is the earliest age to receive Social Security retirement benefits, and for those who choose to retire early, it typically contributes 40% of their pre-retirement income. Full retirement age is when a person is eligible for the maximum benefits, usually 67 if born after 1960. However, individuals who choose to retire earlier face a reduction in their benefits.

Several elements, such as the amount of contributions made during working years, are used to evaluate a person's eligibility for Social Security benefits. As you decide the level of other retirement income you will need to maintain your lifestyle, factor in the expected benefits for the year and then decide how much you must save.

The amount you will need to save is in part determined by the amount of time you expect to live in retirement and the amount of annual income necessary to live in ease. According to the Special Committee on Aging of the U.S. Senate, public health and medicine advances have enabled Americans to live and work for more extended periods.

Most people live between 15 and 20 years after turning age 65 years. By 2026, almost 25% of working age will be more than 55 years old, a rise from 35.7 million people in 2016 to about 42.1 million people in 2026. These changes may allow individuals to save for longer as long as they remain healthy. The following are the three strategies used most frequently to save for retirement:

- Retirement savings, including investments
- Employer-sponsored retirement plans, like the popular 401(k)
- Social Security retirement benefits

Working out how much money you'll need to live comfortably in retirement is crucial when you're making your retirement savings plan. Consider if you have to pay for rent or a mortgage and how much.

For retirees to stay at the same standard of living, they often need 80% of their pre-retirement salary. Given that people live longer than ever, many do not have sufficient retirement savings to support themselves for their remaining years. All families in the working-age have an average retirement savings of about $269,600. This figure is given by the 2019 Survey conducted by Consumer Finance. It shouldn't be surprising that many Americans continue to work past the traditional retirement age out of financial necessity.

Reasons Retirement Planning Is Essential

Steve is a friend who recently inquired about the significance of retirement planning. You might have thought about the same thing or asked someone before. Steve has a good education and has done well in his career. He, like many others, is busy and doesn't feel he has enough time in the day to make one of his most significant decisions.

Though he didn't start retirement planning at first because of shortage of time and being overwhelmed but quickly realize how important it is for everybody, for many good reasons.

To start with, retirement may last far longer than you think. According a report by Tr. Upasna Sunil Wadhwani in 2021, a 65-year-old woman that is married has a 50% chance growing up to 90 years. That is indeed longevity! If you are ready, that is a great news. However, such longevity can be horror if you didn't plan for it.

In fact, in 2022, the average Social Security payment will only be around $1,550 per month, which isn't nearly enough for many people to maintain their pre-retirement standard of living.

Benefits from your Social Security don't offer you enough income for an enjoyable retirement. Government medical care, which caters to seniors, don't cover the cost for many seniors.

A 70% chance exists that someone turning 65 this year will require long-term nursing care. Women typically require supportive care for over three years as they get closer to death.

Having a good strategy for attaining an achievable objective for retirement savings is highly valuable. You have a better opportunity of retiring well and use your income sources wisely to live your desired life.

What is the significance of retirement planning?

Better Health Resulting From Lower Stress Levels

Money matters often lead to a lot of anxiety. The American Psychiatric Association has revealed that more than 70% of people are bothered about money. This abnormally could harm their physical health. Diseases such as diabetes and high blood pressure are linked to financial stress. Money problems might result to worry. It can rob you of peace of mind that you need to enjoy life.

Taking action today to get your retirement plan on track is a critical step toward total financial well-being. This will benefit your physical and mental health.

Spend Less On Tax

Paying more taxes than necessary should not be encouraged. Unfortunately, if you aren't careful, retirement is when taxes can wipe out a significant portion of your income and savings. Planning helps you to get around those taxes.

Start working on a retirement strategy in your working years. Know also that the tax strategy you have in your working years will change as you retire.

You may not have control over your income sources when you are working, but your payment may be relatively stable. Thus, finding allowances and tax reductions to lessen your available pay is recommended.

The contribution you make to your 401(k) plan my reduce your taxable income. This will invariably save you money if you're still working on growing your retirement savings.

You could even be eligible for the Saver's Credit, which can help you pay less in taxes. Depending upon your changed gross pay and documentation status, you could receive a special tax break of 10% and half of your retirement reserve funds.

Furthermore, you'll desire to know how to reduce your income tax for the state. It's more likely you'll be able to reduce your taxes if you have a good control over your sources of income. From the angle of taxation, you should have three income sources in your retirement if adequate plan is put in place.

Know that having multiple income sources is bound to save you lots of money in taxes since it will be difficult to predict future tax policies.

Helps With Making A Better Financial Decision

As you become older, life throws a lot of questions your way. Most of the time, the solutions aren't black and white. You begin to ask questions such as the following.

Is going after a new career path needful in your life? Should you remain engaged to your current employer or move on to start your own business? Can you afford to a luxury home in choice locations

All of these questions have an impact on your finances and should come with a good plan in place. Understanding where things are currently with you regarding your retirement plan helps with making critical decisions for your life.

Enjoy Your Marriage

Money plays a key role in divorce. This should not be a surprise. Misdirected financial goals, too much debt, and not willing to work towards a common financial objective all end up in marital discord.

When partners agree on retirement plans, you take care of key conflict areas in your relationship. When money is taken away from the retirement needs, you should be a ble to concentrate on more important things like where you'll want to reside after retirement.

Forced Early Retirement Shouldn't Scare You

If you have a plan to retire at 55 or much earlier, that is fine. But getting forced out of your job is not. It is unfortunate that more than half all retirees are forced to leave their job. Also, some small amount of employee had to leave their employment to care for their aged loved ones or partner.

You'll be placing yourself in a better position if you plan to leave work at early age with a good plan in place.

Even if you already haven't built your retirement savings, keeping some money aside will give you more time to make a new plan if retirig early is important.

You Won't Be A Burden To Your Loved Ones And Children

From an article by Mark Fonville, in the covenantwealthadvisors.com webpage, about 44% of middle-aged people who have children have not less than one parent that may need care. In the same vein, 15% of today's sandwich generation members financially support their parents and children.

Saving for medical expenses and expected long-term care bills is part of a comprehensive retirement strategy. When you know your bills are covered, you won't have to rely on relatives to make up the difference.

You Can Be A Great Grandparent

A good retirement plan will prevent being a burden to others and offers and provides you the privilege of being a great mother.

Will it not be beautiful to have the family go out on a yearly vacation?

Even if the modesty on a factor for your grandparenting ambition, having enough income enables you to visit regularly and attend occasions as needed.

Prevent Running Out of Money In Retirement

There can be many things that frighten someone. Being able to live on your asset for the remainder of yur life is one. Have a good plan for your retirement is important because it can help you avoid hardship when it comes to finance when you are old.

With your retirement plan, you can know how much you can withdraw from your purse, the amount of risk you may take and the amount of return you require from your investments.

Working with a reliable financial advisor, will help you have sufficient savings stored up for your use. This will prevent you from having a bad time during financial downturn.

Retirement Planning Steps

You can get a safe and enjoyable retirement. Retirement planning changes over time though a multistep process. Thinking about the goals of your retirement including how much time it will take you to accomplish them is a planning step you need to consider first.

Thinking about retirement goals and how much time it takes to accomplish them. The next step is to investigate the various kinds of retirement accounts that may be able to assist you in acquiring the funds necessary to pay for your foreseeable future. To allow that money to grow, you must invest it as you save it.

Taxes are the final stage of planning. If you have received tax deductions for the money you have contributed to your retirement accounts over the years, you'll pay a significant tax bill when you take those savings out. While saving for the future, there are ways to reduce the impact of the tax on your retirement while continuing the process when you actually stop working.

But first, you need to learn the five steps that everyone, regardless of age, should take to create a solid retirement plan.

How Much Savings Do You Need for Retirement?

Someone will require a solid understanding of the amount of money that needs to be saved before they can begin calculating their retirement objectives. Usually, this will rely upon many situational factors, for example, their yearly pay and the age when they intend to resign.

Although no set amount of money should be saved, many retirement experts offer general guidelines like saving about $1M or 12 years' worth annual income before you retire.

Another recommendation is the 4% rule. The rule states that retirees should spend no more than 4% of their retirement savings annually to ensure a comfortable retirement. It's a good idea to sit down and figure out the best retirement savings for you because everyone's situation is different.

Factors To Consider

It's essential to consider a few things that will affect your retirement goals as you plan. For instance, what do you prepare for your family? Starting a family is a primary aim for many, but having children can also significantly reduce your savings. As a result, your retirement plans will consider the family you want.

Similar considerations should be given to your retirement plans, including any alterations to your residence. Traveling adventure may eat into your retirement savings, though it may be an adventure sort of.

However, relocating a nation with a low living cost may enable you use your savings well as you keep to a high standard of living.

Finally, one should likewise consider the various categories of expense-advantaged retirement accounts. Social Security benefits are available to most Americans, but rarely cover all their retirement costs. The next steps in retirement planning are as follows, considering these elements:

1. Know Your Age Range

An excellent retirement plan is built on your current age and anticipated retirement age. You can invest the majority of your funds in less secure endeavors, such as stocks, if you're young and have about 30 years till retirement. Stocks will be erratic, but typically perform better in 10 years.

Additionally, it would help if you had returns that outpace inflation to maintain your purchasing power in retirement. You've all heard — and need — compound development on our cash. In other words, inflation is similar to compound anti-growth in devaluing your money. For approximately 24 years, the value of your savings will decrease by 50% at a rate of 3%, which may appear to be low.

Even while it might not seem like much each year, over time it makes a big influence. Your portfolio should be more heavily weighted toward capital protection as you gain experience. This entails putting more money into less hazardous investments, such as bonds, which won't yield as much as stocks but will be less volatile and pay a living wage. You won't be that much concerned about inflation. A 64-year-old professional who wants to retire the following year does not have the same concerns about rising costs of living as a much younger professional who has just started their career. You ought to divide your retirement strategy into several components.

Consider a scenario in which a parent wishes to relocate to Florida, fund their child's education until they are 18, and then retire in two years. Two years before retirement, saving for and paying for education, and living in Florida (regular withdrawals to fund living expenses) would be the three phases of the investment approach. To determine the best portioning strategy, a multistage retirement plan should coordinate various time horizons and assess liquidity requirements. As your time horizon changes, your portfolio should also be rebalanced over time.

Tips: Saving a few dollars here and there in your 20s might not seem like much, but the power of compounding will make it much more valuable when needed.

2. Determine Your Retirement Spending Essentials
You can determine the required size of a portfolio if you have realistic expectations regarding your spending patterns after retirement.

Many people understand that their annual spending will range from 70% to 80% of what they did before retirement. Adults who are retired no longer need to put in more than eight hours a day at work, so they have more time for expensive pastimes like shopping and traveling. Precise spending objectives for retirement help with planning because higher spending in the future needs higher savings today.

Your withdrawal rate is one, if not the most important, factor in the longevity of your retirement portfolio. Because it'll affect how much you withdraw each year and how you invest your account, it's critical to estimate your retirement expenses accurately.

In addition, you might need more money than you anticipate if you intend to buy a home or cover your kids' college costs after retirement. These expenses must be accounted for in the overall plan. To make sure that your funds remain on track, keep in mind to revise your plan once a year.

3. Calculate Your After-Tax Investment Returns Rate
After determining the predicted time and expenditure requirements, it is necessary to evaluate the true after-tax rate of return to see if the portfolio can produce the required income. Even for long-term investing, a required rate of return in excess of 10% before taxes is typically unattainable. Because most low-risk retirement portfolios are consisting of low-yielding fixed-income securities, this return threshold decreases as you age.

Assuming no taxes and preserving the portfolio's balance, a person with a $400,000 retirement portfolio and $50,000 in income requirements rely on an excessive 12.5% return to survive. The portfolio can be expanded to ensure a reasonable rate of return, which is a primary benefit of early retirement planning. The expected return would be much more manageable at 5%, with a gross retirement investment of $1 million.

Investment returns are typically subject to taxation, which varies by retirement account type. As a result, an after-tax basis must be used to determine the actual rate of return. However, determining your tax status when you take money out is a crucial part of retirement planning.

4. Adopt Estate Planning

Estate planning is part of a complete retirement strategy. Life insurance is also a crucial part of the retirement and estate planning processes. If you have life insurance and an adequate estate plan, your assets will be dispersed according to your wishes and your loved ones won't experience financial hardship following your passing. A well-considered plan also aids in avoiding the pricey probate procedure.

Another crucial component of estate preparation is tax planning. If a person chooses to leave assets to family members or a charity, the tax implications of either gifting or passing assets through the estate process must be compared.

A typical investment strategy for retirement plans aims to maintain the portfolio's value while generating returns that cover yearly living expenses adjusted for inflation. The portfolio is then given to the deceased person's beneficiaries. It'd help if you talked to a tax professional to choose the best plan for the person.

CHAPTER 2

HOW DO YOU STOP BOREDOM IN RETIREMENT?

What Is Boredom?

A bored person doesn't choose to have anything to do. They desire stimulation but cannot connect with their surroundings. This state is an unengaged mind.

That explanation suggests the solution is easily accessible and ties boredom to activity. Put another way, and you can ease boredom by altering your routine. However, it never is. There are times when things happen that are out of your control. Or a partner might have broken up with you, leaving you feeling alone, stuck, and bored.

You may experience periods of both euphoria and anxiety. In a negative cycle, your mind may keep going in circles, making you eat or drink too much to deal with these emotions. Playing games of chance, buying things you don't need, watching television for hours, or even sleeping too much. These activities may now take the form of browsing the internet or looking for entertainment in digital media.

These experiences can provide brief relief from these activities that seek novelty. They might keep you from looking further at what's vital in your life. You're blocking the way to your emotional awareness by constantly ignoring your feelings of boredom and being distracted. Your problems can only be resolved if you are aware of who you are.

The Way Out

Eliminate Your Avoidance Strategies

Begin a behavioral detox by eliminating your most readily available sources of distraction. You can start by limiting your television viewing or social media usage. Your next step might be to alter your sleeping patterns. This continues until you have handled every factor that stops you from dealing with your boredom. You may then start introducing additional positive activities, such as going to the gym or a stroll in the park.

Submerge Yourself In Nostalgia

Allow yourself to reflect on the past. Nostalgia is related to observing your life from a different viewpoint. Memories may transport you back to when you felt more energized and alive and when life had more significance. This may be an excellent opportunity to arrange old photographs. This may bring up memories of old hopes and ambitions.

Reach Out To The World

We sometimes become a world of strangers, turning away from one another out of need, not knowing that boredom thrives in solitude. You may believe that no one cares about you. No one may call or visit you any longer. It will take some work, but you must take the initiative to call, write, and interact.

Find Your Purpose
Boredom can be harmful. When bored, you might engage in unhealthy behaviors that could hurt your health or shorten your life. It poses a more significant threat if it prevents you from experiencing fulfillment in the future.

Finding a purpose will help you forget boredom more quickly and effectively than anything else. During your 60s, you might not have any career plans. This is a great time to look into the passions and interests you may have had in the past but never pursued.

Start by asking yourself what you enjoy most. You can begin looking for something that motivates you by taking small steps. Try to find something that captivates you, even if it takes time. You'll be in a flow state when you can work on something for hours without lifting your head. There is no room for boredom when you are wholly engaged in this manner.

Practice Mindfulness Daily
It's hard to stay in the moment. Our many obligations and commitments constantly pull us in all directions. However, it's essential to remember that being present keeps our lives full of excitement, depth, and flavor.

The capacity to know, be careful, and draw in with what's happening around you can assist with advancing your connections and developing associations with others and yourself. These are only a few of the advantages of mindfulness.

Nobody said it better than Paul

Staying in the now wherever I go has helped me combat boredom. Surprisingly, as a result, I have been engaging in pleasant and sometimes profound conversations with people I have met, such as a grocery store cashier or a nearby exerciser at the fitness center.

It's time to live in the now and stop looking back or worrying about your fears or your retirement future.

Find Your Adventures

What do you do when you're bored? Most of the time, you watch TV, look on Facebook, or watch Netflix simultaneously. If any of this depicts you, now is the right time to step beyond your usual range of familiarity and search for experience and imagination in retirement to dispose of fatigue.

In addition, assuming that anyone is aware of Ella's courage after retirement.

To make up for the time she has lost, she has been working on projects that have required her attention for a long time.

Ella's loved ones are always unsure what she will do next, but she has never been bored.

Even if you don't like flying, you should find a way to get out of your comfort zone and have your adventure at this crucial time.

Engage In Community Roles

Social interaction is vital. Not only does it assist you in surviving retirement without becoming bored, but it also enhances your health and overall well-being. When you're part of a small community, you'll always have someone to lean on and talk to about your experiences.

Nobody knows this better than Mark:

"I began changing and finding where my bliss was the point at which I began going through the Local area."

Mark began making companions from varying backgrounds and became a more grounded, seriously cherishing patriarch to his loved ones. He frequently talks, encourages, and ministers to friends through life's ups and downs as he walks the neighborhood, hills, and trails. Without a doubt, Mark's numerous fellowships and connections are extensive and significant.

In addition, it's essential to remember that connecting with other people for lighthearted entertainment and playing board games, card games, or a straightforward Hearts game online can have several beneficial effects. No matter how light or heavy the interaction is, it's worth it.

Pursue Your Passions

Retirement can occasionally feel like a loss. You lose your job, identity, and the daily routine that once made you happy.

The fact that most people retire relatively early in their lives worsens this feeling. You have many years of discovery and possibilities ahead of you. It's expected that the number of people who live to be 100 by 2050 will rise to 3.7 million.

The good news is that there are ways to avoid boredom in retirement for longer. One way is to pursue hobbies from your youth or discover new ones.

Robert runs a modest business that sells board games and comic books. His vocational way was astonishingly enhanced. He has interests beyond his company, even in retirement.

In his spare time, he manages a blog about retirement.

Working after retirement has advantages and disadvantages. The critical action is that, assuming you choose to work, seek after your interests and incline toward your motivation.

Make New Friends
Stop isolating yourself. Get acquainted with websites like www.meetup.com and make new friends. It's free, and you'll meet others who share your interests and hobbies. You'll find groups to join, such as guitar pickers, cycling groups, etc.

Volunteer

Have you attempted various things to occupy your leisure time but still felt a hole deep down? Many retirees question how to keep themselves engaged in retirement. However, it's more than simply keeping occupied. Finding hobbies that offer you a feeling of purpose and fulfillment is critical. Giving back is also essential.

Shella is an excellent illustration of the advantages of volunteering. For her, it goes beyond simply getting rid of boredom.

She has made new friends and improved her health. Check out volunteer websites to get a head start on your quest for the perfect volunteer activity.

Explore The Luxury Of Unstructured Time

If you're bored in retirement and seeking to arrange your time, you may be missing the point of retirement. A routine is entirely unnecessary. Allow yourself the luxury of time by letting go of the job mindset.

There is no 'wasting' time in retirement. You do anything you want whenever you want. There are no agendas, timeframes, or anything else. Your whole retirement life is now free time. Try the no-plan strategy. It works perfectly!

Stay Active

Jane loved taking part in a local running class when she was in her 50s. However, life got in the way, and her daily exercise routine was at an all-time low.

Fortunately, she had had enough of being told that she was too old to be active by age-related myths. In the wake of heeding guidance, Jane shares some brilliant counsel that applies to both actual work and retired life overall.

Your attitude is everything. It starts with awareness and clarity and ends with action and consistency. It's never too late to move. Start slowly and in increments.

Continuity and the formation of habits are the most important. No matter how old you are, you can successfully alter your relationship with exercise, become fit after 60, and regain your joy in movement with the right attitude and a little knowledge.

Be Accountable To A Loved One

Pat relies on his friends to ensure that he achieves the things he desires to accomplish. And that helps him with retirement boredom. "I'm discovering I need to exercise control of what I practice by encouraging others to join me," he stated.

Contribute Your Unique Skills

If you have a skill that could be useful, why not pass it on to other people? Just follow Lina's lead, a dedicated person who has found different ways to help the world.

She has many passion projects and keeps busy with various organizations and causes. Assisting the less fortunate is one of her most consistent sources of happiness. It's great to volunteer, but if it's important enough for me to do so, I think it's essential, in my opinion, to bring others along so that the activities continue," she says.

Are you easily bored? Are you bored occasionally or regularly? What activities do you take to avoid getting bored? What have you attempted to do to cope with boredom more healthily?

CHAPTER 3

STAYING BUSY IN RETIREMENT, JOBS YOU CAN DO?

Volunteering and working part-time are great ways to keep busy when you're retired. Not all retired folks need to 'rest'. They also don't always want to spend their retirement doing what they enjoy. Some retirees choose job hunting after retirement because they want to be physically and mentally fit or are eager to pursue a new employment sector. They are adopting a lifestyle choice that will affect their long-term health and well-being.

In addition, not everyone who retires has the financial means to live off their pensions and savings. Part-time employment is a terrific method to augment retirement and savings goals with additional income.

Retired people can access numerous paid and unpaid opportunities. A few retired seniors even begin a new profession all together! Retirement doesn't need to be prohibitive. Please pay attention to how you want to use it and what you need to do to get where you want to go in your next life phase.

Part-time Work Types

Many people launch small enterprises and start new part-time or self-employed occupations after they retire in a variety of industries, such as needlepoint, knitting, furniture restoration, and gardening. Start with your passions if you want to work for yourself but are unsure where to begin.

In the current digital era that we live in, the internet has unlocked a lot of doors. This means that if you were a secretary in the past, you may provide firms with remote bookkeeping or typing services. Alternatively, you might enjoy visiting bonanzas and discount sales and have a flair for discovering inexpensive products you can quickly resale online to earn extra money. Options and possibilities are endless!

Self-employment

If you want to work for yourself but don't know where to start, start with your interests. When they retire, many people set up small businesses and begin new part-time or self-employed careers in various fields, including needlework, knitting, furniture restoration, and gardening.

The internet has opened so many doors in the digital age we live in now. This means that if you used to be a secretary, you could offer remote bookkeeping or typing services to businesses that don't have the money to hire a full-time employee. Alternatively, you might enjoy going to bonanzas and cheap sales and have a knack for finding cheap items you can easily resell online to make extra cash. There is no end to possibilities and options

List all your skills, personal qualities, and interests if you like working for yourself. The extra pay you source will assist with your monetary planning and retirement arrangements.

Staff Employment

Older workers shouldn't be forced to do certain kinds of work by law, even if they have retired or are close to retiring. As a result of anti-discrimination legislation passed in 2006, people who are retired or nearing retirement can continue working in the jobs they have held for most of their working lives well past the typical retirement age.

Contact your local Job Centre if you want a part-time job. It'd help if you had the same chance of finding work as everyone else now that age discrimination is against the law.

What about former coworkers? If you want to keep working part-time in your chosen field, networking gives you possibly the best chance of finding work.

Voluntary Work

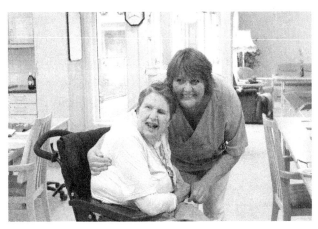

Volunteer work can be a good way for retired people to give back to the community and assist others. They can do this on their own or with a partner who is also retired.

Volunteering has a bucket-load of advantages for everyone involved. It's an opportunity for retirees to meet new people and acquire new skills. It can also be highly satisfying and give your day a sense of direction and purpose. Volunteer work is mentally as well as physically enjoyable. Some recognize it for various benefits, including combating depression, boosting self-confidence, maintaining fitness and health, and cultivating happiness.

Because of their maturity, many charities and volunteer organizations actively encourage retirees to take part; a wealth of knowledge and dedication to the cause.

If you're good with words and a "people person," working with underprivileged youth or offering phone support service might be right up your alley. If you have a car, you may get a job picking up the bags of clothing left outside for charities or driving patients to and from hospitals. Ask about volunteer opportunities at your local government, newspaper, and library.

There are various online resources. Enter "voluntary work" in your local area into a search engine like Google.

Volunteering is a great way to get involved in something you love. Whether it's a pastime, keeping up with your present job, all helps with maintaining engagement in retirement.

Retirement should not mean mingling with only a few close friends. You have a variety of possibilities, such as starting a self-employed business based on your interests and hobbies or working as a volunteer for a company on a part-time basis. You will find more retirement-related activities the more you look for them.

After Retirement Part-Time Jobs for Seniors

1. Resort Worker

Working part-time in a favorite resort might make working part-time look more like a vacation for seniors looking for relaxation. Resort personnel provide customer service in various jobs, including concierge, golf course assistants, lifeguards, restaurant staff, and dock workers. They are dedicated to providing excellent customer service and supporting vacationing customers. With an average national salary of $12.03/hour, this job can help you pay your recurring bills.

2. Focus Group Participant

If you're searching for a low-stress career that pays well after retirement, consider taking part in a focus group. They are often hosted at local hotels or conference centers, with small groups of individuals discussing new goods, services, trends, and concerns.

A focus group moderator will lead the conversation, and a note-taker will take notes. After the debate, participants are frequently rewarded for their time with cash or gift cards, depending on what amount of time they contributed to the discussion.

However, you may also conduct paid focus groups online if you choose. A preferred option is Survey Junkie, which frequently promotes focus group opportunities with pay of up to $150.

3. Tutoring

Do you enjoy giving back to the community by assisting youngsters in learning new skills and ideas at school or at home? Consider becoming an online tutor if you enjoy interacting with people and want to influence future generations.

Tutoring is an excellent career for retirees since it's flexible, rewarding, and low-stress. Depending on where you live, instructors can work from home and arrange sessions around their schedule.

Most firms need instructors with a bachelor's degree and a certificate. However, others may teach you on-site if necessary. Furthermore, depending on your seniority degree, many compensate you for all hours performed each week.

4. Pet Sitter

If you're searching for a fun part-time job for retirees and enjoy caring for animals, becoming a pet sitter could be for you. You can care for people's pets while they are away, besides dogs, cats, and other species of animals are others.

This is undoubtedly one of the finest retirement jobs since it allows seniors to leave their homes and earn additional money.

You'll deal with satisfied pet owners eager to spend top cash for excellent animal care. Creating a profile with Rover is also a fantastic place to start.

4. Dog Walker

Most people adore animals but prefer not to spend more time each week caring for them. Because of this, dog walking is one of the best jobs for retirement because the hours are often flexible. You can work as much or as little as you need daily, and you get to spend time with many dogs!

No one can tell what you'll get with a dog. Every walk is unique, hugely compensating for individuals who love investing their energy with their fuzzy companions. Dog walkers generally charge by the number of dogs they watch at once hourly.

With the Rover site, you can sign up for free and start. Because it's the world's largest site for dog walkers, simply creating a free profile will almost certainly get you started finding clients with four-legged friends!

5. Sell Plants

Selling some plants on Etsy is another fantastic low-stress profession for retirees. If you enjoy gardening, this is one of the finest retirement jobs since you may cultivate and sell plants from your own garden, obtain them from neighborhood nurseries, and sell them at markets or over the internet. Plant vendors may establish their rates and hours, making it a versatile and fun alternative.

6. Sell Jewelry

Selling jewelry might be a terrific choice if you have a gift for design and love working with your hands.

You may sell distinctive goods or resale products from other designers using online markets like Etsy.

7. Design And Sell Items

What about creating and selling your products? If so, Printify is an excellent starting point. It allows you to make and sell personalized items like t-shirts, mugs, phone covers, and more. It's a print-on-demand platform that handles printing, shipping, and customer service while you make money.

Submit your designs, select from various items, and establish your prices. This means you can channel your inner artist and begin developing your things without worrying about inventory or delivery issues.

8. Craft Seller

So, if you're a retired person who enjoys knitting, woodworking, or other hobbies that help you make things, this job is perfect for you. Crafts can be sold online, like on Etsy, Amazon and Ebay or at craft fairs; it's up to you to decide which method is best for you.

In either case, retirees looking for a fun part-time job that gives them time to pursue other interests and spend more time with family will love this option.

You'll need to spend some time making your products and look into the best things to sell on Etsy to ensure your products will appeal to a large enough audience. You can still make money on the side and spend the rest of your day doing things you enjoy with friends and family.

9. Furniture Flipper

This is among the most enjoyable retirement occupations that pay well yet are low-stress. It also doesn't need a formal education.

If you're searching for a low-stress retirement job, consider flipping furniture. You can even accomplish this from home if you have the necessary equipment and room in your garage or basement.

Furniture flipping jobs are great for folks who enjoy bargaining at garage sales or estate auctions. Most people get their start as furniture flippers in this manner.

10. Online Friend

Do you enjoy socializing but don't have time to meet new people face-to-face and would not mind being compensated? One of the retirees' most enjoyable part-time jobs is working from home as an online friend, assisting people of all ages in online dating.

Just honestly, it's on a platonic friendship level. You are expected to be accessible during specific hours of the day and your earnings add up to the number of clients you can serve by the hour daily.

Each client will typically pay you to communicate with them weekly or biweekly via email, chat, text messaging, phone calls, etc. It's similar to using a pen pal service but without the hassle of meeting clients in person. The fact that everyone is paid for their time is the best part. Therefore, everyone benefits.

11. Charity Work

Charity workers frequently concentrate on a specific region or problem and consider ways to improve it. You meet new people who share your passion for assisting those in need.

This will be one of the most excellent low-stress jobs for retirees around you since it'll allow you to make a difference in your community. Fortunately, there are several options to donate your time. Notably, you may volunteer around your schedule and take shifts whenever you choose. No additional degrees or unique talents are required.

12. Animal Shelter Worker

Our society's unsung heroes are animal shelter workers. They care for animals whose owners have abandoned or abused them and work around the clock.

The best news is that there are a lot of chances out around here, assuming that you're searching for practical tasks to take care of after you resign. After all, most shelters require part-time employees and volunteers. It's also an excellent choice for people who've always wanted to work with animals but haven't had the chance.

Most animal shelters provide on-site training, so you don't need prior experience to work there. In addition, regardless of your level of seniority, you may frequently receive compensation based on the number of hours worked each week.

13. Tour Guide

For people who enjoy history, travel, and discovering new places, working as a tour guide may be one of the finest professions for seniors over 60. Because no particular certificates or degrees are required, many seniors may accomplish this work on the fly.

Instead, a genuine interest in the areas you're showing them is more vital. You'll be taught all the pertinent information, but your enthusiasm for the subject will guide you and ensure your tour group has a memorable experience.

Begin by inquiring about any prominent tourist attractions in your region, as they may be able to lead you on the proper path.

14. Author

If you've always enjoyed writing, consider becoming an author. Writing doesn't come with much pressure.

The ideal choice is to get a specialist, but on the other hand, the facts confirm that this isn't guaranteed for everybody. If you really want a low-stress job after retirement, it can also add pressure.

Because of this, Amazon Kindle Direct Publishing might be an excellent alternative. You can self-publish your books on this platform, reaching Amazon's millions of customers and keeping at least 70% of the sales for yourself! This is a fantastic way to get your new book out without having to work with publishers.

15. Consultant

Consulting is one of the most widely used to describe a line of employment. Consulting, using the talents and expertise you obtained while working full-time.

For example, businesses frequently have short-term requirements. They often prefer to recruit retirees for these positions since you have the experience to execute a good job but no need for continuous full-time work.

That's why it's a good idea to notify your network that you're open to consulting possibilities. You might focus on the aspects of your previous career you loved the most, allowing you to bypass the more stressful elements.

16. Life Coach

Another of the best low-stress jobs after retirement is working as a life coach, either locally or remotely, depending on whether you prefer to work in person.

Because it involves assisting other people with aspects of their lives, it's a beautiful opportunity to draw on your previous experience. Alternatively, you could concentrate on topics that have nothing to do with the professional backgrounds of you or your clients. Many people are looking for life coaching in areas of their lives outside of work.

Communication and the capacity to listen will both be essential in this situation. Even though having some expertise can help you gain credibility, this will be far more important than any background you may have in the areas of concern of your clients.

CHAPTER 4

HOW DO I MAKE MY RETIREMENT MORE EXCITING?

Whether you're looking for a new hobby or want to relax on the patio with your morning coffee, retirement provides an opportunity to reset your rhythm. The secret is to figure out what you want to accomplish, avoid long periods of boredom, and focus on what's important to you to make the most of the future years.

Here's what you should do in retirement to make your life more interesting and exciting.

Clean up your living space.
Examine your closets, desks, drawers, and cabinets. Long you're at it, climb up into the attic and arrange everything you've been wanting to do for a long time. Keep everything that is good where it belongs and sell or distribute the remainder. Knowing that everything in your possession is in order and that you are just carrying what you absolutely need will give you piece of mind.

Research Your Family Tree

Do you want to know your descendants, where your ancestors lived, and what they did? Researching your family tree is now easier than ever owing to many internet services such as Find My Past. Examine census data, military records, and passenger lists for relatives who have traveled the world. You might even incorporate your children and grandkids as a continuing family in the line.

Stay Fit

Start an activity that involves light body movement, such as Tai Chi, golf, yoga, pool, bowling, croquet, or archery. All of these workouts focus on building core strength to strengthen the body and enhance overall fitness and wellbeing.

Go For A Part-Time Job

Having a part-time work can be quite beneficial because while some people are incredibly self-motivated, others find it harder to maintain a routine when they don't have to.

There are some fantastic part-time employment available for retired professionals who have a wealth of knowledge and expertise from many years working in a corporate environment if you wish to work from home. As a part-time consultant, you get compensated for sharing your knowledge. It's a great choice for businesses since it enables them to access knowledgeable guidance without having to spend money on a full-time staff. Look for freelance opportunities on websites like Upwork to increase your clientele.

Stay Social

Staying in touch has never been easier, whether it's checking up with friends on Facebook, starting a WhatsApp group for women, Skyping your family overseas, or chatting online with an old friend in another country. You may communicate with friends and family anywhere in the globe whenever you like if you learn about social media and the newest internet communication tools.

Be Financially Savvy

Align your new way of life with the money you make each month. If you pay more than expected in one area, look for methods to cut costs elsewhere.

Commit To Your Health

You may now devote time to a healthy lifestyle with the extra hours. Acquire a watch or use an app that tracks your sleeping patterns. Going outside most days and keeping up with your medical visits might also help you feel better.

Take On A Different Hobby

There are several options for people who desire to enhance their artistic aptitude, ranging from sketching to sculpting. Crafts, cooking, sewing, and foreign languages are covered in online courses, videos, and e-books. You also have access to local expertise, such as a pianist who teaches on the side or a potter who gives regular workshops.

Think About Relocating

Think about moving to a retirement home if you want to be near other elders. Those who reside in northern states may feel compelled to travel south during the colder months. Relocating closer to family or a lower-cost-of-living place may suit your lifestyle choices. If you're undecided about where to live, try it out for a few months before deciding.

Focus On Your Style

Retirement frequently necessitates a shift in daily attire. Those who enjoy fashion and apparel may want to pay attention to blogs and influencers who appeal to the 50 and older population. It may imply a shift to more informal and comfortable clothing for others.

Discover Local Attractions

Retirement allows you to explore your neighborhood if you've spent most of your vacation time traveling or visiting family. Local restaurants, festivals, fairs, and historical locations may all have distinct attractions.

Get A New Pet

Pet owners are typically happier, more trusting, and less lonely, according to pet researcher Allen R. McConnell of Miami University. They also go to the doctor less frequently for minor issues.

When you're lonely, a pet may be an excellent company source. According to research, having a pet can help reduce anxiety, sadness, and cardiovascular problems.

Adopting a cat or dog has the added benefit of keeping you active. Maintaining a pattern of feeding and walking your pet may also offer structure to your routine and add to your overall feeling of purpose.

Prof McConnell suggests one explanation for this might be because your pet gives you a sense of belonging and significance. "You have a better sense of control over your life."

Visit your local animal rescue center, the RSPCA, or Dogs Trust to learn about pet rehoming. Contact The Cinnamon Trust if you're interested in helping to walk or foster an older adult's dog.

Try Something New

It's easy to get trapped in a rut, both physically and mentally, and trying something new can be a pleasant change. Some people have discovered that making minor adjustments, such as trying a new dish, going to a new hairdresser, or enrolling in a new fitness class, may give them a new lease on life.

CHAPTER 5

WHAT YOU CAN DO ALL DAY WHEN YOU'RE RETIRED

According to 2019 American Time Use Survey statistics, retirees have more than seven hours of free time daily. They use their free time doing some things, such as picking up new hobbies, resting at home, watching TV, and pondering everyday events. Many retirees work or volunteer after they retire. Here's how American retirees spend their time.

Sleep

Those who have worked for decades are deserving of the right to get more sleep. Older people and children have the most fantastic time for rest and other personal care duties. People aged 75 and up spend 9.9 hours sleeping and caring for themselves daily—people under 25 spend over 10 hours daily when sleeping, showering, and dressing. The rest of the population sleeps a little less.

Shopping

Retirees have the leisure to compare prices and visit many places to find the most incredible offer. Finding needs at an affordable price is becoming increasingly vital for folks on a budget. People aged 65 to 74 spend the most significant time shopping in person, on the phone, and online, spending about an hour daily. In comparison, people aged 35 to 44 spend three-quarters of an hour shopping on average.

Working

Many people work over the age of 65. On average, those aged 65 to 74 work for a little more than an hour every day. This estimate includes income-generating side enterprises such as selling homemade crafts, babysitting, keeping a rental property, or holding a yard sale. However, older individuals eventually cease working, and for seniors 75 and older, time spent earning money decreases.

Volunteering

Some retirees use their leisure time to give back to the community. Retirees spend more than a half-hour each day volunteering or participating in other civic or religious activities, much more than the quarter-hour paid by those aged 35 to 54. This estimate includes working for a charity, attending religious or spiritual events.

Exercising

Retirees have few excuses not to exercise, yet most retirees aren't devoting more time to staying fit. When people first retire, there appears to be a slight rise in time spent exercising, from 13 minutes for those aged 45 to 54 to 15 minutes for those aged 55 to 64. However, for individuals 65 and older, exercise time declines to a mean of 13 minutes each day.

Reading

Retirement may be a time to read those intriguing novels you've meant to read or get lost in the contemporary thriller. Older folks have more time for reading than younger people. People aged 65 and up spend the most time each day flipping pages, roughly 37 minutes.

Relaxing

Stepping out of the workforce allows you to unwind finally. Retirees have the advantage of having more time to rest than any other age group. People aged 65 and over spend about 30 minutes daily relaxing, compared to 19 minutes for all Americans aged 15 and up. One of the finest aspects of retirement is the freedom to envision and accomplish things at your speed or to do nothing at all.

Socializing

Maintaining a social life in retirement might help you feel connected to your community. Older adults connect with friends and neighbors for around 40 minutes each day, roughly the same length as younger ones. Face-to-face social contacts, as well as hosting or attending social activities, are examples of this. In addition, retirees spend an average of 13 minutes each day playing games, which may be sociable if you play board games with others.

TV Watching

The most common leisure activity among seniors is watching television. According to U.S. Bureau of Labor Statistics data, people 65 and older watch 4.6 hours of TV daily, compared to around two hours for people 25 to 44. People aged 55 to 64 watch more TV before retirement, with a mean of 3.24 hours of watching television each day.

Exploring The Internet

Older people may now use the internet just as much as younger people. Retirees use computers for pleasure and recreation at roughly the same rate as the general population. Retirees also communicate with others for approximately 15 minutes daily via phone calls, letters, and email.

Meals

Retirees do not need to rush over breakfast on their way to work. Those who no longer have to work long hours have more time to look for nutritious meals or meet their friends for lunch. Retirees eat and drink for 1.35 hours daily, lingering for a few minutes longer than the general population. As individuals become older, their time spent eating and drinking improves gradually but consistently.

Home Maintenance

Many retirees want to improve their houses, and those 65 and older spend the most time doing so, over two and a half hours daily. Older adults devote substantially more time than younger people to lawn and garden maintenance, home repairs and renovations, cooking, and cleaning. The time spent on domestic duties progressively rises with age, from one hour in the early 20s to slightly over two hours in the late 50s and early 60s.

CHAPTER 6

67 FUN THINGS TO DO IN RETIREMENT

After working your entire life, the prospect of having plenty of spare time seemed almost too good to be true. A lack of responsibility, a carefree attitude, and limitless leisure may sound like an ideal dream right now, but after a year or two or three out of employment, many retirees find themselves bored and with nothing to do. Don't allow this to happen to you! There are several strategies to avoid boredom and enjoy your golden years.

Do you want to know how to have fun during retirement? We're here to provide some suggestions. Here are the top 67 things to do when you're retired and bored, including insights and statistics from other retirees!

1. See The World, Travel

In many retirement wish lists, traveling ranks near the top. Some retirees have always wanted to visit a particular city. A more regular travel schedule is significantly more exciting for some.

Great travel experiences can be had without crossing oceans. You could see everything in North America while traveling through it. Even traveling within your state can give you opportunities you didn't know existed.

Travelers lead varied lives. Some people enjoy taking the train. Naturally, flying will take you almost anywhere. Retirees can be inventive when it comes to lodging. You could try Airbnb, a service that connects travelers to private homes and breakfast experiences in the United States and worldwide.

You could even think about becoming an Airbnb host and renting out your home as you travel the world, making your home your source of income.

2. Go On To Summer Camp

Summer camp is not only for children. It's just as much fun in retirement as it was when you were younger. The grown-up version is more likely to provide various experiences that far outnumber any "wilderness" camp you may have experienced as a child. There is an adult camp for fishing, fitness, racing, car driving, acting, and other activities.

If you have an interest, chances are there is a camp for it. What about a spa retreat? Adult centers may be found on SummerCampHub. The possibilities are intriguing. There is a camp for everything.

3. Relocate Seasonally

Traveling south for the colder time of year is not a groundbreaking thought, yet what we might say about going north when the intensity is excessive? You might want to live near your kids more often, but not always. Or, if you've never spent the holidays at the beach or in the mountains, that's also a possibility.

You can have everything you want without giving up your roots by purchasing a vacation home in another location.

Try swapping homes.

House swap services match you with another homeowner who wants the opposite, and you temporarily swap houses if you're in the north and want to go south. International house swappers also exist. Try HomeExchange.com and HomeLink.com.

4. Grow A Garden

Working outside in pleasant weather makes life worthwhile for some people. Research shows that gardening might add years to your life.

Gardening may take various shapes. Some individuals enjoy cultivating vegetables, while others enjoy the beauty of a flower garden. You can do both. There is so much to learn about plant cultivation. If it's your passion, you may grow new plants, become an expert at composting, or nurture roses and veggies to sell at a market.

5. Write A Book

A low-stress activity like writing can be ideal for people who have just retired. Finding a pace and style that suit your needs and way of life is crucial. That would entail scheduling an hour of writing time each day for some people. Others might just have a little window of time each day, or they might choose to write in short bursts as they get the opportunity.

6. Don't Allow the Age You Are To Rule You

Age is just a number. It should not define your retirement activities. Look at these incredible feats by 70, 80, and 90-year-olds and other extraordinary accomplishments showing that growing old are genuinely optional! Recall that Pablo icasso kept on creating paintings in his 90s. At the age of 84, Thomas Edison created the telephone. Keep moving and doing things you love to do.

7. Remodel Your House

Retirement is an excellent time to remodel if you want to retire in your own house or even sell it. You may change your home to accommodate a new lifestyle or enhance it to increase its worth and receive a higher market price.

Improvements may include a new first-floor main bedroom, a safer bathroom, kitchen renovations, a hobby studio, or whatever else your heart wants. This is also an excellent opportunity to ensure your home is in perfect shape. If you need a new roof, replacing it now means you'll have fewer worries later.

8. Learn To Play An Instrument

Even if you don't think you've a musical bone in your body, you can discover an instrument that you enjoy playing. Piano and guitar are trendy places to start. Remember that your voice is also an instrument. You may also take vocal classes. Not only can learning to play an instrument enhance your life, but it's also an endless endeavor. Even the world's best musicians practice and learn new things regularly. Learning new things is also an excellent strategy for maintaining your brain's health.

9. Raise Your Friend Base

Too frequently, retirees cling closer and closer to home as time passes. What may have been a large group of friends may decrease until just a handful remain in your life. While there's nothing wrong with spending time alone, having friends keeps you linked to the world and gives you a sense of purpose. Finding some younger pals is also an excellent idea. Spending time with someone of a different age group exposes you to fresh experiences and vice versa.

10. Attend Your 40th High School Reunion
You will most likely be attending multiple reunions. Don't skip them if you want to stay in contact with old friends, coworkers, and relatives.

Nothing compares to a high school reunion to get you thinking about what you've done and where you want to go. As we face retirement, we must take stock of our life and develop new goals. A reunion may be a great chance to reconnect with old friends and get reminded of what we're passionate about, which can help us decide how we want to spend our retirement.

11. Hang Onto Technology

Generation Y is the first to have grown up in a world where the internet has always existed in some form or another. Older generations had a lot of life experience without it or any of the standard technologies. Keeping up with technology throughout retirement provides a lot of flexibility and allows you to reap more benefits than living in a quickly developing environment. Accept technology and continue to study.

12. Spend Time As A Grandparent

"Perfect love does not come until you have your first grandchild," a Welsh adage states. If you're seeking things to do in retirement, consider activities you can do with your grandkids. Being a grandparent is an incredibly fantastic experience. You receive all the child's love. You may share essential experiences with children and learn about topics that are important to them. They can help you stay youthful, and you can help them mature.

13. Visit Family & Friends

It's an excellent time to see your loved ones again. You don't have a job that limits the number of vacation days you may take. Spend the week or month with your friends or family as you like.

14. Cook More Frequently

One of the easiest and most cost-effective activities after retirement is cooking more at home. You'll not only eat healthier, but you'll also broaden your appetite by trying different flavors and recipes.

15. Explore Your City

Even if you've lived in the same place for decades, chances are you've been too preoccupied to keep up with the current trends. Take this opportunity to admire your hometown and learn about what has changed since your previous visit.

16. Join Adult Programs

In terms of cities, find out whether your city has any specialized senior centers or activities.

17. Learn A Language

Learning a new language has never been easier. There are many low-cost classes available both online and in person. You could even do this for free with all the free language learning materials available on the internet.

12. Explore By Rail

Board a train and experience up to six magnificent rail adventures throughout North America. When you're over 60, you get a 10% discount.

18. Frequent Coffee Shops

Sip tasty blends from famous coffee shops around you in the afternoons. This inexpensive pastime is ideal for mingling or enjoying the city's peace.

19. Adopt A Pet

More than half of Canadian families have at least one pet. So, if you don't already have one, why not spend your leisure time with an adopted pet? It's less expensive than you think. And it's a great way to share the love with a pet – especially from animal shelters.

20. Visit Museums

There are several fascinating museums in all around the world. You can visit them to learn more about art, nature, and culture. The best thing is that if you're over

65, you may obtain entry or membership discounts in most North American countries.

21. Start Scrapbooking

It's the ideal moment to revisit old memories and make new ones. So, why not create a scrapbook to compile old and new memories into a physical record of your life's journey?

22. Explore Nature

Exploring outdoors is one of the most affordable ways to have fun as a retiree. Try wandering through parks, mountain hikes, or kayaking on the Great Lakes. For the finest experience, enjoy nature throughout the seasons.

23. Try Meditating

Another beneficial exercise for reducing stress and improving mental health is meditation. Meditation requires no special equipment, so give it a shot at least once. You can attend in classes in person or online.

24. Watch Movies In Cinemas

Instead of viewing movies at home, go to the Cinema. It's a fun way to interact while eating popcorn.

25. Create A Vision Board For Retirement

This practice is comparable to setting yearly objectives, but it's more creative. To picture how you want your retirement time to appear, cut out magazines or print photographs. When you can see your goals, it's simpler to achieve them.

26. Learn To Save A Life
You have no idea what could happen at home or in public settings. To respond swiftly to situations, learn life-saving skills such as CPR or first aid. Many organizations, like the Red Cross, provide courses that will teach you to save lives for less than $200.

27. Adjust Your Daily Routines
A constant daily regimen from Monday through Friday is no longer required. Feel free to change your patterns based on your mood or aims.

28. Discover Your Neighbors

You may have been too busy to interact with your neighbors before, but befriending them now is an easy way to maintain social interactions. So engage in small talk or invite your neighbors to a summer barbeque session.

29. Try New Restaurants

The cosmopolitan climate of the Americas fosters a diversified cuisine scene. Try various eateries whenever you have time as a fun way to learn about different cultures while interacting.

30. Enjoy Some Mean-time

Choose an engaging interest that's only for you if you enjoy passing the time of day quietly in your own company. Learn how to work with some stuff so you may create your own furniture, decorations, gifts for friends, and items to sell. Create cards with a personal touch. Create beautiful decors. The list goes on and on. Enjoy yourself; you deserve it!

31. Attend Live Performances

Another enjoyable way to spend your spare time is to attend entertainment, such as concerts or plays. Most venues offer senior discounts, making live events an affordable opportunity to engage with the arts and your community.

32. Write A Journal

Start or end your days by keeping a journal. It has been proved that writing down enjoyable experiences improves your general mood.

33. Propagate Plants

Propagating your plants will help you improve your gardening abilities. Collect low-maintenance house plants to try this pastime inside.

34. Watch A TV series

Start a TV series if you've trouble overcoming daily ennui. Netflix features scores of titles that span many seasons. Starting one can keep you busy for several days, if not weeks.

35. Try New Teas

Most of us begin our days with hot tea or coffee. Experiment with fresh flavors or mixes of your favorite drink to excite your mornings.

36. Start DIY Projects

Take on new DIY projects to reconnect with your creative side. You could discover new hobbies while saving money on new purchases.

37. Play Video Games

You may have been too preoccupied with your profession to experiment with video games. Now you have the leisure to recapture your childhood with this ever-changing type of entertainment.

38. Be Sporty

Playing sports is one economic and enjoyable activity for retirees. Regardless of your fitness level, a try is always waiting for you.

39. Enjoy Festivals

Participating in festivals is one of the most enjoyable things you can do after retirement. It serves as a breeding environment for music, cuisine, and socialization. When it comes to having fun at festivals, age is only a number.

40. Offer to Dog-walk

Walking dogs is a terrific stress-relieving part-time job if you love animals. You get to meet new hairy companions every day, and if you've a good customer base, you may raise your charges.

41. Become A Pet Sitter
Another way to supplement your income after retirement is to work as a pet caretaker. You'll get compensated for feeding, cuddling, and watching pets do tricks or sleep all day. Isn't it amazing?

42. Bake And Sell Desserts
Selling baked goods is one of the quickest and most fun methods for a retiree to make money. Sell your masterpieces to friends, family, and neighbors to earn additional cash while having endless treats in your cupboard.

43. Become A Photographer

Become a photographer to turn your pastime into a job. You have the option of marketing your service or selling photographs.

44. Setup A Garage Sale
Kijiji and Facebook Marketplace are the internet's equivalent of garage sales. List your used items on platforms like these to earn money with no effort.

45. Be A Film Extra
Why watch movies when you can be a part of them? Apply for extra work through talent agencies or casting websites. Earn money while learning about how movies are created behind the scenes.

46. Birding

If you enjoy nature, bird watching is a beautiful activity after you retire. This activity also provides healthy doses of sunshine and fresh air; if you invest in some basic equipment and binoculars, it's one of the few free activities! That's beneficial for your mind and your wallet.

47. Cooking

This is your chance if you've always wanted to channel your inner cooking skills. Choose a good cookbook and experiment with different dishes, or watch your favorite cooking shows on TV.

48. Join Book Clubs

According to a recent survey, reading material such as magazines and eBooks has the highest percentage rise in household spending (71.3 percent) after retirement. You may pursue one of America's favorite pleasures while interacting with friends by attending a book club.

49. Sell At A Farmer's Market

Sell handcrafted baked goods or plants from your garden at your local farmer's market. It'll provide you with a weekend activity and the ability to earn money for extra travel, books, or whatever retirement passion you like.

50. Sell On eBay

eBay is a terrific way to sell your furniture, elaborate brooches, and other small goods you could discover at a swap meet, but have you considered all the valuables lying around your house collecting dust? From old baseball cards to mismatched dinnerware, you may be relieved to declutter your house and find new homes for your formerly valued items.

51. Take Online Surveys

Getting paid for internet surveys is a low-maintenance method to make money and pass the time during retirement. Although surveys aren't considered a pastime in and of themselves, they may be a rewarding opportunity to have your opinion heard, have an influence as a customer, and earn extra cash on the side.

52. Record Audio Books

Bookworms may elevate their interest by reading their favorite literature aloud. Many businesses pay for audiobook recordings, which need little technical knowledge and a knack for storytelling.

53. Meet Other Retirees

Whether you're 55 or 65, joining social clubs of other retirees is ideal. Taking part in social activities can help you better appreciate this new stage of your life.

54. Go Camping

Camping is one of the most important things to do after you retire if you want the end of your hectic profession to sink in. This calm hobby may be done alone or with friends and family. It's a low-cost way to commemorate the conclusion of your hustling era.

55. Social Organizations

Join meet-up groups oriented toward specific interests or populations. Clubs based on reading, chess, astronomy, or gem and mineral prospecting are excellent options, as are dating websites.

56. Celebrate Yourself

Make a list of your previous achievements and efforts. This is a simple method to remember what has provided significance and joy to your life and how purposeful you are. Once you have this list, you'll most likely understand what you like and want to focus on!

57. Watch The Sunrise Or Sunset

Every day, there are sunsets and sunrises. It costs nothing to view them. Therefore, be sure not to miss any of them. They are breathtaking, and it has been proven that seeing the sunrise or sunset makes you appreciate the planet more. And you're happier and more appreciative of what's taking place in front of you. So, it's a great way to start or end your retirement day.

58. Listen to Podcasts

The modern version of a radio broadcast is a podcast, however instead of being live, it is recorded and accessible at any time. Several podcasts are available that are uplifting and intriguing to listen to. You might browse for podcasts on retirement, your hobbies, or other life issues.

59. Have A Picnic

Go out on a picnic and enjoy the day. Bring a book to read while lounging in the sun, or ask some friends to join you. Look through your kitchen cabinets for foods and drinks. As an alternative, you can buy local products for your picnic from a local farmers' market, which are typically less expensive than those found in a store.

60. Go For A Hike

Nature is accessible to all. Spending time in nature improves mood and emotional condition while reducing anger, fear, and anxiety. By reducing blood pressure, heart rate, muscle tension, and hormone production, it also improves physical wellness. So take a stroll outside; it's free and healthy for you.

61. Have A Bonfire

A good bonfire is the best thing ever. Use free wood material from your backyard or a nearby forest to build a campfire. Grab a guitar and spend the evening singing the night away with some friends who will bring beverages and snacks. You get more at ease when you watch a fire, and it might be the ideal way to cap off a fantastic night in retirement.

62. Pick Fruit

If you are in a bountiful place with lots of fruits in retirement, you can collect fruit like strawberries, apples, or cherries. Find nearby orchards where you may pick fruit or city parks with fruit trees.

63. Go To The Beach

 If you reside close to a beach, you can visit it. There are many things you can do for free on the beach, so if you live in a city, check to see if there is an urban beach where you might spend a day in retirement. You can walk, swim and eat fresh fruits on it as you relax.

64. Go Stargazing

In retirement, going on a stargazing outing is a pleasant and affordable hobby. Find out where in your state is best for stargazing. Get in your car on a clear night, get a few drinks, and a comfortable blanket and take in all that nature has to offer.

65. Write A Letter

Instead of calling, you might send a letter to a friend or family member. Your Christmas or birthday cards can be written well in advance. Or you could start writing to strangers and develop a pen pal relationship. Volunteers are needed by several organizations to write letters to people or kids in need.

66. Create A Video

You might create a video for YouTube or as a surprise gift for a loved one's birthday or anniversary. A camera/smartphone, and a free video editing software are all you need.

67. Do A Puzzle

Does it rain outside? The perfect time to tackle a puzzle is at that moment. In order to play online at jigsawplanet.com or the Magic Jigsaw Puzzle app, dust out those 1000-piece puzzles from the attic and begin.

CHAPTER 7

SINGLE AND RETIRED-
WHAT TO DO

You aren't alone if you intend to retire single. Nearly one in three older adults will live on their own by 2020. Some people may be terrified of retiring without a partner, while others may feel empowered by the prospect. 46% of non-dating singles over 50 don't desire a relationship because they enjoy being single. After all, if you're single, you can live more freely, devote more time to your interests, and avoid arguments over where to eat dinner.

However, retiring alone also comes with difficulties. For instance, if you don't have a partner, you might have to work harder to connect with others, care for yourself as you age, and reach your financial goals.

This section's advice for single people retiring will provide you with all the information you require making the most of your golden years.

Make A Plan For Your Ideal Retirement

It's essential to know precisely what you want from your retirement. You can use this to determine how much money you need to save. When planning your retirement, take into consideration the following:

- What would you like to do in your spare time?
- Where do you want to live?
- How do you plan to keep your health?

Your retirement strategy will change because of your responses to these questions. For instance, if you want to live in a posh cabin, you will probably need to save more money than if you lived in a studio apartment in your hometown. There are courses to get to any retirement objective you could conjure up. Imagine a luxurious retirement that can inspire you to budget and work toward those objectives.

Create Financial Goals

Now that you know your ideal retirement, it's time to get more specific about your financial goals. Everyday things to think about are:

How much money will you need to live comfortably?
How much will you need to put away each year for savings?

What is your current level of debt?

If you have a Visa or understudy loan obligation, one of your most memorable objectives may be to take care of them. If your credit rating doesn't look excessively great, you could make an objective to work on your credit. You'll know how much money you need to retire if you set these smaller goals.

Build Your Emergency Savings

High costs can sometimes appear out of nowhere. Perhaps your car breaks down, you lose your job, or you have a pet that requires surgery. Having a fund saved up in these scenarios is a good idea. A typical amount to save for an emergency is four to six months' pay.

Grow A Support Network

It's no secret that social life is essential for general pleasure and well-being. According to research, social isolation and loneliness might have the same detrimental side consequences as smoking.

Attend events, join communities, or contact old friends or relatives to expand your social network. When you check in with your loved ones regularly, whether in person or via the phone, you may form long-lasting bonds that will survive well into your elderly years.

Consider Long-Term Maintenance Insurance

There's always the possibility that you'll require assistance taking care of yourself at some time. This can be a challenging chore without a companion, which is why investing in long-term care insurance can be beneficial.

Long-term care insurance can help you pay for assisted care and housing if you require continual maintenance. Remember that the younger and healthier you are when purchasing coverage, the less expensive it will be.

Find A Part-Time Job

While you may not want to work 40 hours per week in retirement, part-time jobs may provide your golden year's structure, purpose, and extra revenue. Assuming you're financially secure, your part-time employment can be about doing what you like rather than generating money.

You could wish to try freelancing, becoming self-employed, or entering a new field that interests you. Monitor your mental well-being and ensure that your part-time employment does not interfere with your enjoyment.

Prioritize Estate Planning

Estate planning is especially crucial for singles because you don't have a spouse to help disperse your possessions when you die. While you probably have stuff you'd like to leave to your loved ones, only half those between 50 and 64 have a will.

An estate plan should include funeral arrangements, guardians for your children, and an executor to carry out your wishes. Remember to keep your beneficiary designations in any retirement funds or life insurance plans in your name up to date.

Invest In Annuities

Annuities are a terrific method to ensure a consistent source of income later in life. Because you don't have a spouse to transmit your money to in the case of your death, annuities generally pay more when you're single. Investigate the various annuity kinds to determine which one is best for you.

Choose Someone To Make Your Decisions

As a single retiree, selecting someone who will make health care or financial choices for you is critical if you cannot do so yourself. If you become ill or otherwise handicapped, your desires will still be carried out by someone else.

People typically appoint trusted friends or family as their healthcare proxy. However, the person you name as executor doesn't have to be the same person you call your healthcare proxy. However, the executor should know who the designee is and where the documentation is kept. If no one comes to mind, the next best thing is to fill out a proxy form that outlines the medical procedures you support and oppose.

Choose The Right Place For You

The location of your retirement has a significant impact on the quality of your golden years. For instance, a place you adore might be ideal for a vacation but not retirement. Other interesting points as you pick your retirement area include:

Weather: Which do you prefer, warm summers or cold winters? Do you like to live in a bustling city or close to nature?

Urban life: You might need to go out and meet new people because you're single. Check out the activities and communities in the area to see if it's a place you want to call home.

Cost: It's possible that a location looks perfect but is too expensive for your budget. To pay for living expenses, this could require you to relocate or alter your savings plan.

Assisted living facilities: People who want a community built into their homes can find affordable housing in retirement communities. For seniors who don't have a partner, some communities are just for single people.

When selecting a location for your retirement, you can live alone, with roommates, or in a retirement community. Make sure you know how much money you need to live comfortably in retirement before deciding. This will affect your housing budget.

Experiment With Leaving Your Comfort Zone

Avoiding boredom might be one of the most challenging problems of retirement. While routines might be beneficial, doing extra activities to prevent the days from becoming monotonous is also helpful.

For example, you may try taking a dancing class, preparing a new meal, or going on a walk to overcome your fear of heights.

Use An Alert System

You become more prone to dangerous falls and unanticipated medical emergencies as you age. This can be scary when you don't have a partner to look out for you. Fortunately, virtual assistants like Google Alexa and medical alert systems can safeguard you.

In the event of an emergency, a device known as a medical alert system can connect you to your loved ones or medical professionals. An alert device could be worn as a watch or a necklace, or you could store it somewhere safe and easily accessible.

Do your homework to ensure you purchase a device that fully meets your requirements and comes from a reputable manufacturer before settling on an alert system. For instance, if you are concerned about risk of falls, you might want a device with motion detection that will notify someone if you fall.

Similarly, digital assistants like Amazon's Alexa can respond to statements like "Alexa, I've fallen and can't get up" by asking, "Would you like me to call 911?"

Remember that occasionally these frameworks are sufficient not to protect you. Check out your home health care options to ensure you are taken care of right.

Go On A Date

Love can be found at any age. Even if you're not seeking a serious relationship and merely want to meet someone new over dinner, you'll have lots of time to discover your romantic side during retirement. There are several ways to locate a companion, whether through your retirement community, a standard connection, or online. You might also try senior dating websites like eHarmony.

Keep Your Mind Sharp

As you age, losing a portion of your psychological agility is normal. However, there are ways to help your memory and remain sharp. You might, for instance, want to keep a steady rest plan.

Your psyche's well-being comprises the food sources you eat, the things you do, and the individuals you communicate with. Your brain will always be sharp as a tack if you care for yourself physically, mentally, and socially.

Prioritize Your Health

Maintaining your well-being will keep you happy and allow you to enjoy a long and prosperous retirement. It'd help if you prioritized fueling your body daily with well-balanced meals, physical activity, and cerebral stimulation. It'd help to plan frequent health check-ups to ensure your health is in excellent working order.

Connect With Nature

Connecting with nature regularly can help ease depression symptoms and stress. This is especially important for retirees, because research shows that approximately 2 million senior citizens in the United States rarely leave their homes, which is linked to a higher risk of death.

Thus, making arrangements to interface with nature routinely is smart. Spending time outside can help you feel better, whether you stroll through the park or relax in your backyard garden.

Single life in retirement can be an excellent way to spend your golden years. You will have a life that is both peaceful and satisfying if you put your health first and make financial planning a priority. Talk to a Medicare advisor immediately if you want more information about senior health care.

CHAPTER 8

ACTIVITIES FOR RETIRED ADULTS

Whatever your age, hobbies, or talents, you may find activities that will make you giggle, lose track of time, or feel like a kid. And many activities are inexpensive or free. The following are some of the most effective forms of activities for older adults.

Excursions And Field Trips

Nobody likes staying at home all the time, especially if the home is a busy living space. In the nicer districts, there are special trips and excursions to nearby attractions including museums, orchestras, and nature preserves. Some even work with nonprofit organizations to support senior citizens in volunteering and giving back. A seasonal journey is an excellent opportunity to build memories and a significant experience for both of you if you want something to do with your loved one.

Sports And Games That Need Physical Activity

These allow you to exercise, enhance your eye-hand balance, and acquire control over your surroundings. All of this may be really rewarding, especially if you overcome barriers or compete with other individuals pleasantly. Consider the following examples:

- Golf
- Pool
- Tennis
- Badminton
- Croquet
- Ball tossing
- Volleyball
- Lawn bowling
- Wii Bowling
- Curling

Watch Concerts On YouTube

Seniors are living longer lives than ever before. As a result, they now have more free time at home. It's critical to discover enjoyable and exciting indoor activities for older folks. Here's an idea: watch a concert. YouTube is the right place to do this.

Hundreds of thousands of concert footage from all genres may be on YouTube. You can listen to music by your favorite band or vocalist or see an artist who is new to you but appears to be worth checking out.

Dancing And Other Performances

Dancing to music may help your body connect to both exhilarating and therapeutic rhythms. Singing famous songs (even if you're terrible at it) in front of others might help you laugh at yourself and avoid treating yourself too seriously. Other forms of performance, such as participating in a skit or attempting a stand-up comedy routine, might remind you how much fun it's to tell tales in innovative ways.

Take a chance and attempt something new, such as:

- Line, salsa, ballroom, or swing dancing
- Acting in a play
- Seniors' karaoke
- Telling jokes to a group
- Writing
- Launching a seniors' dance troupe

Organize Photographs

Organizing photographs is one of the most enjoyable and engaging activities for seniors. Having a box of old photos can be overwhelming, but it's a simple project that can ultimately bring you a great deal of satisfaction.

Gather all of your old pictures first. The next step is to sort through your photos according to the subject matter of family, vacation, or pets. You can use other criteria such as by date. Please put them in photo albums or binders once you've sorted them into categories and put them on display where everyone can see them!

Parties And Social Gatherings

Socializing may be a practical approach to add extra enjoyment to your life. This is especially true if you get to reminisce about former times or discuss topics that fascinate you. A good discussion can improve your mood and perspective more than anything else on this list, especially if you keep it lighthearted. So don't be afraid to attend other people's parties or join clubs. Consider organizing some of your own events. You may organize parties based on a variety of themes.

- Casino night
- Trivia night
- Mexican fiesta
- The 1920s, 50s, etc.
- Arabian nights
- Pirates
- Hawaiian luau
- The Oscars
- Secret Santa
- Formal tea

Have A Spa Day

Spa days are a terrific opportunity to treat yourself and spend time with others. Consider scheduling a day at the spa for your senior citizen friends or family members if you want something exciting and interesting to do with them. You may make this as basic or intricate as you like; the choice is yours! You can book everyone into a spa for massages and facials. If you want something more relaxed and low-key, book them into an outdoor hot tub—they'll adore it!

Live Music/Music Therapy

Seniors today are a part of an age that introduced live music and music therapy to a make a difference in the space. Many are still music fans who have very particular preferences. Senior communities provide live music, like concerts by local artists, or cater to this interest. You might even see a resident perform at a concert in a society where musicians once lived.

Absolute healing potential exists in music, especially for those with dementia. Some assisted living facilities hire qualified music therapists to provide small-group cognitive stimulation and entertainment for the residents. In certain places, seniors with musical backgrounds can even offer entertainment or music therapy events to their friends and neighbors.

Traditional Games Plus Puzzles

Board and card games are excellent ways to interact while enjoying the fun challenges of friendly competition. And puzzles may help you strengthen your thinking while providing a sense of progress and success. Consider the following alternatives.

- Scrabble
- Pictionary
- Bingo
- Checkers
- Dominoes
- Monopoly
- Chess
- Go Fish
- Poker
- Bridge
- Canasta
- Rummy
- Solitaire
- Crossword puzzles
- Word search puzzles

Knitting And Crocheting

Knitting and crocheting are both enjoyable and engaging hobbies that persons of any age can enjoy. They're also a great way to keep your hands busy, which is especially important for people with memory problems like dementia.

Knitting and crocheting may appear to be specific crafts, but they can be challenging. For instance, it may be difficult to know where to begin if you are unfamiliar with the various stitches used in these crafts.

A ball of yarn and two needles are needed to knit. The adventure typically has a few strands twisted together to make it easier to work with. You utilize the needles to make circles on one side of the ball while getting through different processes on the opposite side. This results in a knit fabric!

Crocheting uses two needles just like knitting, but instead of using twisted yarn strands like in knitting, you use a single long strand called a "hook" that is hooked into loops at the end of each row by pulling through loops from previous rows known as "stitches".

Animal Interactions

Animals, like humans, seek and require enjoyment. Playing with them may thus be beneficial to both parties. Even if you don't have any pets, it's generally simple to discover animals to engage with. Many animal shelters, for example, accept seniors who wish to spend time with dogs, cats, and other animals.

Gardening And Other Outdoor Activities

Being outside may do wonders for your attitude as long as the weather is nice. After all, the natural world is brimming with pleasing sights, sounds, scents, and other sensory delights. They make you feel like an adventurer or linked to something more than yourself. Consider the following.

- Gardening
- Walking
- Hiking
- Bird-watching
- Picnics
- Boat rides
- Metal detecting
- Kite flying

Arts And Crafts

These creative leisure hobbies are excellent for people of all ages and frequently make unique pastimes. These kinds of ideas may rekindle a person's vigor and feeling of possibility.

- Painting
- Ceramics
- Sketching/drawing
- Mosaics
- clay modeling
- Woodcraft
- Papercraft
- Beading
- Crocheting
- Quiltmaking
- Knitting
- Jewelry making
- Embroidery
- Card Making

Active Learning

Learning is usually more enjoyable when you desire to do it for your education. Whole new channels of possibilities open up. So go with your curiosity and instincts. Learning anything new is helpful at any age. Consider learning how to do the following as examples.

- Sing/ play an instrument
- Write code
- Speak/write a foreign language
- Design websites
- Take professional photos
- Cook exotic meals
- Write great stories
- Perform magic tricks

The activity aspect is probably the best part of living in a senior living community. Residents regularly attend concerts, events, and social gatherings. Senior social activities today are anything but dull. Assuming you or your adored one are resigned and searching for exercises for senior residents that are everything except exhausting, the list above will take care of you. Whether you live in a senior community or at home, take some time to practice them. Remember that connecting with peers can significantly improve mental and physical health. Investing energy in an occasion, making companions, or finding old colleagues can affect your general health.

CHAPTER 9

UNUSUAL THINGS TO DO IN RETIREMENT

What unusual things for seniors might keep them from being bored in retirement? In this chapter, you may locate, try, or learn about them. And whether there's a benefit to your health and relationships or keeping prices low, it's all right here as well!

Why Unusual Hobbies? What makes a side interest unusual? In this instance, unusual can refer to unique, unconventional, or something that is now rarely done. In addition, you can substitute uncommon or even eccentric to be regarded as "unusual".

Alternately, "unusual" refers to pastimes we rarely associate with retirees. Traditional stereotypes are constantly being thrown out the window by Baby Boomers! It very well may be uncommon because of the speed of innovation. Perhaps it was recently created.

My list of forty unconventional hobbies for seniors include:

1. Glassblowing

Glass blowing is gaining popularity more than ever before. Artisans typically perform this skill that has existed for centuries. Artisans can train for decades, depending on the glass being made. Murano glass has been regarded as the best in the world for more than a millennium.

However, the artisans who make Murano glass aren't just hobbyists. They do work in hot shops with large ovens, expensive materials, and skilled workers. Still not convinced that this is an unusual pastime you might want to try?

But don't worry; creatives and artisans are happy to share their expertise and space. Many artisans are opening their hot shops for classes and permitting novices to use their gear, broilers, and materials. With options like these, you can quickly test out this potential activity.

2. Encaustic Painting

Because of the materials used and the time it has been around, encaustic painting is one of the "unusual" hobbies for seniors. Encaustic paint is made from bees and beetles, not from oil or acrylic, which are common mediums. More specifically, a damar resin and beeswax blend is an excellent combination.

It would be an understatement to say that this painting style dates back a long time. Models can be tracked down in Egyptian burial chambers. Encaustic was used to paint the face boards of mummies, which still look great.

There are numerous excellent resources for learning about this kind of art. Encaustic could be the new medium to revive or energize your practice if painting is already your retirement hobby and how you spend most of your time. Collage, sculpture, and printmaking all work well with it.

This is one example of a mixed-media encaustic painting, and it's a strange thing to do in retirement.

3. Jewelry Making

Making jewelry is a massive retirement hobby category. Since the beginning, using gold, silver, and semi-precious stones has been artisanal. Some people are well-versed in the art of silver and gold smithing. For others, it's a craft thanks to hobby stores and cheaper materials.

There are many unusual things to make or materials to work with, regardless of where you stand on the art or craft. Statistics indicate many people enjoy creating jewelry somehow!

It's an inexpensive hobby to begin with. Because it was much less expensive than buying each tool separately, purchase a straightforward jewelry-making kit containing all the required tools.

You may not particularly appreciate making earrings, but bracelets are fun and require less effort than necklaces. There is a class, book, instructional exercise, video, course, or retreat for everything from silversmithing to breastplate-making.

4. Ice Sculpture Carving

It's as hard as any other type of sculpture, but not as durable! Carving ice can be accomplished with hand tools, with several difficulty levels. Even freezing the ice requires real skill.

You might be interested in learning that there are international competitions for ice sculptures. Ice sculpture competitions are from Canada to Japan and China to Sweden. Grab your sculpting tool, snow boots, toques, and winter gloves. Canada is home to three of the top ten events in the world.

It keeps you active, gets you outside in the winter for fresh air, and does all the other things creative art does to stimulate your brain. There is something for every sculptor level; if nothing else works, make a swan for the buffet!

5. Martial Arts

All martial arts are great for fitness and mental and physical well-being. Self-defense encourages mindfulness and lowers stress and independence.

Millions of people practice martial arts for these great reasons. If millions do it, how is it unusual as a retirement pastime? Beginning martial arts much later in life isn't typical. What are the "experts' opinions?"

Some experts say that starting between 6 and 22 is the best time. Michelle Yeoh began at 22, Bruce Lee at 13, and Claude Van Damme at 12. In any case, if you believe you're too old even to consider the beginning, you are.

With good reason, it can be harder to learn martial arts as we get older. But are you doing it so you can hang out with Joe Rogan after an MMA cage fight? There must be one for novices!

6. Dog Sledding

Indeed, dog sledding is a way of life; for some, it's more than just a hobby.

This outdoor activity offers some advantages, including exercise, fresh air, and the company of man's best friend. Geography will play a role if you want this to be a regular retirement pastime. However, besides enjoying riding the sleds and caring for their dogs, dog sledding enthusiasts also engage in other hobbies like hunting and fishing.

Instead of flying, hunters frequently use dog sleds to reach remote campsites. They come in handy when you're packing out what you've caught or trapped. Dog sledding is more "hobby-like" for some people.

7. Paintball

Paintball isn't a royal sport! However, you may do it outside with your friends or grandchildren. Think wisely and keep your head down. What's not to love about this? If you will, those friends and grandkids become your team, tribe, or unit.

There is enough data to suggest that being a part of something good for you and allowing you to be your best self is beneficial. That's why this section included paintball on the list of unconventional activities for seniors. It's because you're doing it for scientific purposes!

8. Lamp Work

In the 14th century, lampworking spread widely in Murano, Italy. Then, in the early 17th century, traveling glassworkers made lampworking more accessible to the public by demonstrating it to them. What precisely is a lampwork?

It's the art of making tiny art objects out of small pieces of glass, usually beads or other embellishments for jewelry and decor. Even as far back as the fifth century B.C., there are a few examples.

A great way to improve an existing hobby of making jewelry and often serves as a prelude to glass blowing.

Regardless of the method, retirement may be the ideal time to experiment. Marbles are the most significant advantage. Marbles were once made using lampwork.

9. Brewing Beer

In theory, it's not a hobby or something unusual. How recent is it? Ancient! Beer in the Ancient World claims it dates back as much as 10,000 years. It's brewed traditionally by women rather than men.

At first, people consume it with a straw, which is now prohibited! Those are only a few of the information in the article. Rewind to more recent information.

Craft beer brewing has a remarkable history, and craft beer brewers are preserving a centuries-old tradition lacking in today's consumer society.

What advantages are there to making your beer? Pride. You can keep your mind sharp by learning materials science, mechanics, and process. However, consuming an excessive amount of your science project can negate that advantage. According to some, brewing your own beer is a fun and economical way to save money.

10. Puppetry

Puppetry? Isn't that for youngsters? Yes generally. Kids will often appreciate watching puppetry more than grown-ups do. However, what if there was more to puppetry than simply "watching it"? Could we include puppetry on the list of unusual hobbies for seniors because of another aspect?

This pastime has lots of advantages, including preserving skills, giving back to the community, and keeping your brain sharp through creativity.

CHAPTER 10

CHEAP THINGS TO DO AT RETIREMENT

As per a new review from the Transamerica Community for Retirement Studies, one major fear about retirement is tracking down significant ways of investing energy and remaining involved in active life.

For some, it's a matter of money. Health problems or problems in the family can drain a lot of money. As a result, some could not save as much money as they would have liked because they were forced into early retirement.

It's a question of identity for others. Retirement can be a scary time if your job title has always defined you. Luckily, many exercises are modest, and engaging in something new can assist you with manufacturing another character.

This goes beyond simply remaining active and engaged. It could also imply surviving. A study published by JAMA Network Open found that adults over 50 who didn't feel like their lives had meaning were more than twice as likely to die between 2006 and 2010.

Here are some low-cost ways to prolong your golden years.

Cook Healthy Meals

Making nutritious meals is a fantastic place to start when taking care of your health as a retiree. Enjoy this exercise by trying different cuisines and creating your own meals.

Take Daily Walks

Taking daily walks keeps you active and energized. For further cardiovascular advantages, stroll at your speed or try fast walking.

Join A Fitness Class

Your health is more important than ever. Participate in a fitness class near you. Alternatively, if you want to exercise in the privacy of your own home, look for courses online.

Take Up Yoga

Yoga is a low-impact workout that is ideal for elders. Purchase a yoga mat for as little as $12. Then, watch YouTube videos or enroll in official seminars to learn more about this activity.

Enroll In A Gym

Purchasing a gym membership is a simple method to keep yourself accountable for your health. Gyms provide a secure location to try new workouts and gain confidence as a senior.

Join Fitness Contests Online

Fitness challenges are shared on social media. Try one to keep active, and if you find a challenge too difficult for your fitness level, feel free to make changes.

Try Diverse Dance Styles

Dancing isn't merely one of the most enjoyable retirement activities. It's also a great way to keep active and healthy. To stay fit, try out different dance styles and exercise your body.

Cycling

Many cities are incredibly bike-friendly. Consider Vancouver, which has 400 kilometers of bike lanes—cycle into and out of town to exercise while taking in the sights.

Go Hiking

Hiking is one of the finest ways to appreciate varied landscapes while staying healthy. You aren't required to trek challenging hills right away. Begin with picturesque hikes on gentle hills and gradually increase the challenge.

Stretch

Flexibility aids in the prevention of injuries as you age. Join stretching sessions or watch basic internet tutorials to stretch your muscles.

Swimming

Swimming is another low-impact exercise that is ideal for seniors with delicate joints. Try paid or free community lessons in this sport and bring other retirees to make it more enjoyable.

Try Winter Activities

Aside from skiing, try ice skating and snowshoeing to get decent exercise without becoming bored.

Mentor A Younger Person

The fortunate ones among us received professional guidance, encouragement, and advice throughout childhood and perhaps even beyond. Why not show the same kindness now that you're retired?

This could mean helping a young person transition into adulthood or supporting someone entering the same industry as you did. Anyone who wants to work with minors can expect being screened for suitability. The number of hours required varies.

Some mentors find their mentees through organizations like Big Brothers, Big Sisters, service clubs, or churches. You might get in touch with people looking for advice through a professional group you used to belong to. Alternatively, you can check out MENTOR, a non-profit that might assist you in locating a young person who might benefit from the perspective and advice of an adult.

Try mentoring once in a while if you have the time. Giving back this way feels great because the difference could change someone's life.

Have A Potluck Party

If you enjoy socializing in retirement, you may hold a potluck or, as some call it, a BYO (bring your own) party. It might be a dinner where everyone provides a great self-cooked meal or a movie or game night where everyone gets snacks and beverages. It doesn't cost you anything, you have a good time with your friends and family, and you usually have some leftovers you can eat the next day.

Go To The Library

Aside from books, your local library offers many other advantages. You may rent movies, read publications, or browse the internet. There are also several volunteer possibilities. A library's atmosphere may be both motivating and comforting.

Visit Museum/Zoo During Entry Fee Days

Call a nearby museum or zoo and inquire about free entrance days. As a senior, you generally get a discount, but sometimes you may go in for free. Many museums provide free entry or "pay what you can" admittance one day every week or month.

You may also inquire whether they provide complimentary passes on request. Alternatively, local libraries can lend out museum passes for the day. Once you're aware and do some research, you'll typically discover several options to experience museums, zoos, and science centers for free.

Cook Different Recipes With Leftovers

Make an innovative recipe out of your leftovers. Alternatively, go through your kitchen cupboards and see what you can create with what you discover. Perhaps this retirement finding will result in the creation of a new legendary family dish.

CHAPTER 11

WHAT NOT TO DO IN RETIREMENT

If you plan, you may avoid these blunders and save your retirement. There are things you shouldn't do during your retirement. You must be realistic about your expectations and how you intend to prevent the most common retirement blunders.

1. Failing To Budget

Do you recall that you have a fixed income now? In retirement, some costs decrease.

Medical expenses. Medicare does not cover all costs. Depending on your choice of Medicare coverage, you may be required to pay for most dental work, including glasses, hearing aids, and others. You must ask for help if you cannot maintain the yard or deep clean.

Your children are occupied with their own lives, so you can't expect that they should use one of their valuable days off every week doing outside tasks in addition to your cleaning and clothing. This could be an additional expense that must be added to your budget.

Food. Ingredients could quickly become expensive if health conditions necessitate specialized diets. And if your health issues make it hard for you to cook, you might have to rely on meal delivery or takeout, which are much more expensive than making meals from scratch in your own kitchen.

It simply implies you want to live with a sensible spending plan, as when you were working. You can keep track of your monthly spending on paper or with a service like YNAB (You Need A Budget), which makes the process easier and automates it.

If you're afraid to use your retirement accounts, spending too much could cause you to withdraw too much or put yourself in debt. Make sure to budget appropriately.

2. Undisciplined

As you approach retirement, you become excited about almost everything opposite to that hotly anticipated day. When the time comes, you'll stay up late for a week or more, enjoy around the house, play golf, or do whatever you always did for entertainment and relaxation while working. You might even go on a few trips to celebrate. However, you will eventually experience severe existential anxiety upon awakening.

You had no idea how much you would miss your job's structure, expectations, and anesthetic comforts. Humans are creatures of habit; for many, who they are and what they define who they are. When you experience anxiety, it's time to move beyond the initial vacation phase of retirement and consider your plans.

Write your thoughts and aspirations, research, investigate your interests, and plan a course. To put it another way, make a wish list. Create new, healthy routines that give you structure and prevent you from feeling like you're stumbling aimlessly through life.

3. Spending Fixed Income On Your Grown-up Kids

Naturally, you wish for the best for your children. However, sometimes assisting them might jeopardize your comfort and safety in the long run.

For instance, young people are increasingly staying in the family home in their 20s and even early 30s. Yes, some offer to pay the rent, but some parents decline.

Parents frequently continue to assist their children, even when they are alone. The Pew Research Center says that parents are helping to pay for necessities like utilities, mortgages, and financial emergencies.

Take a hard look at your finances before you help your kids or grandchildren. Is that harsh? What's harsher, having to call those adult children ten years from now and say, "I can't pay my basic bills." Please send me some cash.

4. Don't Downsize Your Home so Soon

When you resign, offering your home and moving to more modest accommodations is enticing, particularly assuming that you want cash. However, you might want to put this on hold if your payments are low or you have paid off your mortgage. Things to think about.

It is costly to downsize. Even if you're just moving to a retirement community on the other side of town, the actual move can be expensive and emotionally and physically taxing.

Consider that you would leave behind old friends, everything familiar, and probably family if you are considering a long-distance move to what we regard as one of the best areas for retirement in the nation.
After retirement, if you put off moving to a new house, you won't have to deal with as many changes simultaneously.

There are less stressful ways to put your equity to use than selling your home if your monthly housing costs are low and you need more money. You could rent a room or the garage as a studio to make money.

5. Never Blow Your Savings

After retirement, most people live on a fixed income far lower than they earned while working. With so much free time, blowing money like you're on vacation is tempting. Budgeting and financial planning are essential. Enjoy yourself, but only use your funds for your needs. Save money on products and services.

Sell everything you're not using. Take charge of your credit. Make the most of your senior citizen status. When traveling, use your wits and keep track of your expenses.

Reducing your expenditure may take some time, so try to avoid impulse purchases. Keep your receipts and don't remove sales tags until you've determined you need the thing you've just purchased.

6. Becoming Sedentary

A lot of individuals fantasize about relaxing in retirement. You would instead not take it excessively simple. A variety of health issues can result from a lack of exercise.

The Public Foundation on Maturing, part of the U.S. Division of Wellbeing and Human Administrations, reports:

When older people lose their ability to perform tasks independently, inactivity is frequently more to blame than age. A lack of physical activity can increase medical visits, hospitalizations, and medication use for various illnesses.

Energy, physical strength, balance, and sleep, all benefit from physical activity. It can help you reach or keep a good weight, diminish pressure and nervousness levels, work on mental capability, and oversee or try to forestall specific sicknesses.

Promising to remain dynamic isn't sufficient. It would help to have a real plan, like a daily date to the mall with friends or a health club membership. Colleges and recreation centers might also be good places for low-cost exercise options.

7. Never Be Afraid To Put Your Hands On New Things

Convert an interest into a new profession, acquire a part-time job, volunteer, return to school, or take a class. Experiment with new stuff! Developing your entrepreneurial spirit or learning something new is never too late. These may provide some much-needed structure to your life, soothe any restlessness, and open up new social channels.

You'll have a good time and meet new people of all ages who share your hobbies, plus your soul, mind, and spirit will enjoy it. You could discover a passion that will give your retirement years meaning and purpose.

8. Never Neglect Your Appearance

Ageism exists, particularly among women, but it can also be an internal mentality. Yes, you are retired and getting older. Your body has changed, your hair is thinner and grayer, and you will never look the same as in your 30s or 50s. However, there is no reason to let yourself go just because you are older and no longer need to look your best for work.

Maintaining your exercise routine is as important as caring for your skin, nails, and hair. Although it may be more complex and take longer when you are older, retiring means you have more time to devote to your beauty and fitness routines.

9. Don't Give Up On Romance

Love and intimacy are essential to happiness, especially for your health, happiness, and overall well-being after retirement.

That's wonderful if you're married. Your relationship with your spouse will change, but you can get out of the housemates' behavior, get to know each other again, have some new fun, and rekindle love and romance with just a little time, effort, and understanding.

As we mentioned earlier, there are a lot of sexy senior singles, and being single doesn't mean giving up sex. Most of them are dying because they don't have a loving companion. Putting yourself out there might be challenging, but if you want someone special to share your golden years with, you'll have to go prospecting for a friend.

Therefore, gather your strength, rise to the occasion, and go prospecting. Interfacing with an old or new love is more straightforward than at any time today on account of the web. You could join a senior dating site like eHarmony or look for your old flame on Facebook or Classmates.

If someone catches your eye, talk to them or invite them to lunch or a cup of coffee. Remember that figuring out what you want and asking for it's essential to getting what you want. Don't be shy or afraid to put yourself out there.

10. Give Too Much

Giving is said to be more blessed than receiving. But what if your giving grows beyond control?

Rather than destroying your funds, make "beneficent giving" part of your financial plan. That could be a particular percentage, like a 10% church tithe. Alternatively, you might consider the figures and give it a fixed amount, say, a $120 limit per month.

Whenever you've arrived at that sum, stop.

Research a cause on websites like Charity Navigator or GuideStar before donating. You'll know how much goes into helping other people. It's admirable that you want to help. However, you want to deal with yourself before you can help any other person.

CONCLUSION

When paired with appropriate financial resources, robust physical and mental health, and fewer duties, the golden years often provide possibilities for self-fulfillment, meaningful participation, and achievement.

People retire for various reasons and at different ages during this period. There're no set plans for how to spend your retirement years. Retired people's lives are as diverse as the people themselves. When you're retired, you can do whatever you want within boundaries. However, during that critical and delicate shift, there will always be an adjustment time and understanding of what to do and what not to do.

Boredom is a significant roadblock for many retirees to enjoy their retirement. This book has helped guide seniors who have retired from active work to continually stay active and live a fulfilling life. By reading this book, you'll have seen the many fun things you can do in retirement to keep busy and live a happy life after work-life. The lists and guides offered in this book are not exhaustive. Feel free to add your opinions. I hope that doing so will help you, in the long run, add more value to what we already provided in the chapters given.

THANK YOU

Just wanted to let you know how much you mean to me.

Without your help and attention, I couldn't keep making helpful publications like this one.

Once again, I appreciate you reading this book. I absolutely enjoyed writing it, and I hope you did too.

Before you leave, I need you to do me a favor.

Please consider posting a book review for this one on the platform.

Reviews will be used to help my writing.

Your feedback is extremely helpful to me and will help me to generate more. upcoming books in the information genre.

I would love to hear from you.

Terrance.

Printed in Great Britain
by Amazon

23174355R00079